KU-613-399

The National Trust for Scotland

COMPLETE IN TEXT AND PICTURES

by

PETER
RYAN

J. M. DENT & SONS LTD
LONDON

© Text, Peter Ryan, 1969
© Map, J. M. Dent & Sons Ltd, 1969

All rights reserved. No part of this publication may be reproduced,
stored in a retrieval system, or transmitted, in any form or by any
means, electronic, mechanical, photocopying, recording or otherwise,
without the prior permission of J. M. Dent & Sons Ltd

Made in Great Britain
at the
Aldine Press · Letchworth · Herts
for
J. M. DENT & SONS LTD
Aldine House · Bedford Street · London
First published 1969

SBN: 460 03874 5

The

National

Trust

for

Scotland

5

Contents

List of illustrations, vi
Author's Note, viii
Publisher's Note, ix
Introduction, x
Index, xiii

———— ⌐⌐⌐⌐ ————

v

Illustrations

vii

Author's Note

In pictures or text, or both, this book, in a single volume covering the whole of Britain or in five separate area parts, complete to the end of March 1969, deals with every property of the National Trust in some degree, from a full entry down to a listing by name. Each illustration is accompanied by a description of the property illustrated, and also, in some cases, by notes on other properties near to or associated with it. Thus the text accompanying an illustration of a bay or headland may include notes on several properties in the district from which the illustration is taken. Other properties, which are not illustrated and are not mentioned in the texts which accompany illustrations, are referred to in the appendix covering the relevant area.

When writing the texts which accompany the photographs, I set myself the following guidelines. I would say what in my opinion are the most notable things about the property; give a brief factual account of what the visitor sees there; and give a report on any aspects of its history or of the history of people associated with it that may help the visitor to understand the interest of the place.

I apologize to architects, botanists, art historians, archaeologists, ornithologists and the many other specialists whose studies can be enjoyably pursued on Trust property, if I have failed to bring forward what are to each the most significant points. Please treat these notes as a menu, which even in the best of restaurants can provide no more than an indication of what is available. To be proved and enjoyed, the pudding must be eaten.

Names italicized in the texts are of features not already referred to in the heading to the text, that are (1) illustrated in the accompanying pictures, or (2) illustrated elsewhere in that or another area part, or (3) referred to in the relevant appendix.

I am indebted to Mr Philip Sked, publicity officer of the National Trust for Scotland. He placed his knowledge of their properties at my disposal, and his enthusiasm and love for them encouraged and helped me in a most agreeable task. Although he has generously volunteered to accept blame for any deficiencies or errors in the Scottish part of the book, they should in fairness be charged to my Sassenach pen.

1969   PETER RYAN

Publisher's Note

The author and publishers are grateful to the National Trusts, the publishers and the photographers acknowledged, for their indispensable aid in the preparation of this book.

As an aid to visitors, an approximate location is given at the head of each entry and on the maps provided. It is assumed that the intending visitor will be equipped with his own road maps, also with the National Trust publications *National Trust Properties* and *The National Trust for Scotland Year Book*, which give more precise locations. The present book is intended not as a guide-book but as a complement to a guide-book.

Unless otherwise indicated with the description of the property, or unless it is obviously closed (e.g. where it is leased to a private body), the property is open to the public at certain seasons, days and times.

Using the Trust publications, *National Trust Properties Annual Opening Arrangements* and *The National Trust for Scotland Year Book*, intending visitors should always check opening times in advance, since they frequently change. This is the reason why opening times are not given in this book.

A small number of properties that appear in the appendices will not be found on the maps: they are recent accessions, obtained by the Trusts too late for inclusion in the maps. Approximate locations are given in the appendices.

Introduction

THE NATIONAL TRUST which operates in England, Wales and Northern Ireland has been in existence since 1895, and the National Trust for Scotland since 1931.

Both work on the same lines, and their object is to preserve places of historic interest or natural beauty. They are independent charities; that is to say, they are not under government control and have the legal status of charities. They are run by their own members, subject to the requirement, contained in the National Trust Acts, that half the members of their councils must be nominated by other bodies. The present lists of nominating bodies include museums, universities, the Royal Institute of British Architects, scientific societies, the County Councils Association and the Youth Hostels Association.

Service on the councils and on the committees which run the Trusts' affairs is voluntary. Each Trust employs a paid staff which deals with day-to-day property management and accounting, and includes specialists in matters with which the Trusts are much concerned: gardens, for example.

The Trusts are dependent financially on voluntary support which they receive in the form of donations, legacies and members' annual subscriptions, membership being open to all.

The National Trust was founded at a time when, although both the Society for the Protection of Ancient Buildings and the Commons Preservation Society had been established for a number of years, public interest in preservation was far less widespread than it is now. Also, there were, then, no Town and County Planning Acts as we have them today. Sir Robert Hunter, Octavia Hill and Canon Hardwicke Rawnsley, who were effectively the founders of the National Trust, had been active in campaigns to prevent unsuitable development, notably on Wimbledon Common and in the Lake District. They decided that the time had come to form a society which could act as a holding body, in appropriate cases, for buildings and lands which rank for permanent preservation. In framing the constitution of the society and defining its objects they were remarkably far-sighted. The National Trust was registered under the Companies Act in 1895 as a non-profit-making company. In 1907, when it had grown in public confidence to the extent that Parliament recognized the importance of its work by passing the National Trust Act of 1907, the constitution of the 1895 Society needed no amendment. Nor has it since been altered, subsequent legislation affecting the Trust having been designed to facilitate its work, not to amend its constitution or powers. When the National Trust for Scotland was incorporated by statute (in 1935) the Confirming Act followed closely the provisions of the National Trust Act of 1907.

The history of the Trust's work in furthering the aims so clearly established by its founders is a record of growth. This growth has not followed any recognizable pattern, but it has been a continuous process. The first acquisition—by the gift of 4½ acres of cliff-land at Dinas Oleu above Barmouth in Merioneth, overlooking Cardigan Bay—was made in 1895. By 1967 the total acreage in the Trust's ownership had grown to nearly 400,000 acres (approximately the equivalent in area of the county of Hertfordshire). The figure for the National Trust for Scotland was 74,000 acres on the mainland. In the same year the list of buildings, gardens and other places which are opened to the public at stated times and on payment of an admission fee contained 257 entries, and that for the National Trust for Scotland, thirty-two.

Some properties have been acquired after public appeal for funds for their purchase. Gifts of property have been made not only by private individuals and some commercial and industrial firms, but also by local authorities, many of whom in addition help the Trusts by making grants towards the upkeep of Trust properties. Since 1946 there has been a further important factor in this growth. In that year the Treasury was empowered, when accepting buildings or lands in payment of death duty, to transfer them, with the Trust's agreement, to the ownership of one of the Trusts. Among the well-known places acquired by the Trusts in this way are Hardwick Hall, Brodick Castle and Brownsea Island.

Membership of the Trust, which in 1968 was 160,000 (that for the National Trust for Scotland being 37,000), has grown mainly in the years since 1945. Before the 1914–18 war and during the 1920's and 1930's, although numbers increased each year, the rate of increase was very small and total membership of the National Trust in 1939 was under 10,000.

As property owners the Trusts have one unique privilege—they are empowered by the National Trust Act of 1907 and later legislation to declare land inalienable. Such a declaration having been made, the property is protected against compulsory purchase by local authority or by a ministry; it can only be taken from either Trust by special will of Parliament.

From their beginnings the Trusts have regarded themselves as trustees for the nation, and for that reason adopted the name 'National Trust'. For that same reason the public have access to Trust properties; it is not restricted to Trust members. At many properties a charge is made for admission and the proceeds put towards upkeep. Access to open spaces is usually free but is always subject to the needs of farming, forestry and the protection of nature.

In deciding what should interest them, i.e. what constitutes 'historic interest or natural beauty', the Trusts take a very broad view. As this volume shows, the properties which they have accepted for protection include industrial monuments, nature reserves and prehistoric sites as well as historic buildings of interest and beautiful countryside.

RESTRICTIVE COVENANTS AND RESTRICTIVE AGREEMENTS

In addition to being a property owner, the National Trust has been given or has bought restrictive covenants over some properties which are not in its ownership. These covenants are legal agreements which provide, for example, that alterations to the exterior of a building may not be made without the Trust's consent. The covenant continues despite changes in ownership. Thus it affords a useful measure of protection for the appearance of the property under covenant.

There is, however, an important difference between the legal position of land owned by the Trust and that of land under covenant. Under the National Trust Act of 1907 the Trust has, as explained above, the power to declare its land inalienable. Land under covenant is not eligible for this unique protection.

There is also an important difference in regard to public access. Subject to the needs of farming, forestry and nature protection, there is access to all properties *owned* by the Trust. But covenants do not include any provision for access, and visitors are not usually admitted to covenanted land.

In Scotland the term 'restrictive covenant' is not used, but the term 'restrictive agreement' covers very similar arrangements. The National Trust for Scotland is party to a number of such agreements.

Index

5

THE NATIONAL TRUST
FOR SCOTLAND

St Kilda, Western Isles: gannets off St Kilda.

St Kilda

There are two sides to the Trust's preservation work in the St Kilda island group—on the one hand the preservation of the wild life of the islands, and on the other the study of the way of life established there during the long period of occupation before 1930.

The Trust organizes periodic expeditions to the group, which has been leased to the Nature Conservancy.

The picture below shows a *cleitt*, one of several different styles of construction of which specimens are being preserved. The cleitt was a combined store and drying chamber. The turf roof is thick and keeps out rain; the drystone walls let through enough wind for drying purposes. A cleitt might have contained food, fuel, nets and clothes.

St Kilda, Western Isles: a cleitt.

Key

SCOTLAND

1 Abertarff House, Inverness
2 Bachelors' Club, Tarbolton
3 Balmacara
4 Balmerino Abbey
5 Bannockburn Monument
6 Barrie's Birthplace, Kirriemuir
7 Ben Lawers
8 Binns, The
9 Blackhill, Stonebyres
10 Boath Doocot
11 Brodick Castle, Isle of Arran
12 Bruce's Stone, New Galloway
13 Carlyle's Birthplace
14 Charlotte Square, Edinburgh
15 Corrieshalloch Gorge
16 Craigievar Castle
17 Crail
18 Crathes Castle
19 Culloden

20 Culross
21 Culzean Castle
22 Cunninghame Graham Memorial
23 Dollar Glen
24 Dunkeld
25 Fair Isle, Zetland
26 Falkland Palace
27 Folk Museum, Glamis (Kirkwynd Cottages)
28 Gladstone's Land
29 Glencoe and Dalness
30 Glenfinnan Monument
31 Goat Fell and Glen Rosa, Isle of Arran
32 Grey Mare's Tail
33 Hamilton House, Prestonpans
34 Hermitage, The
35 Hill of Tarvit
36 Hugh Miller's Cottage
37 Inveresk Gardens
38 Inverewe
39 Kintail
Kirkwynd Cottages, Glamis: see Folk Museum, Glamis

40 Lamb's House, Leith
41 Leith Hall
42 Linlithgow, houses on High Street
43 Menstrie Castle
44 Mote of Mark
45 Pass of Killiecrankie
46 Phantassie Doocot, East Linton
47 Pitmedden
48 Pittenweem
49 Plewlands House
50 Preston Mill, East Linton
51 Provan Hall, Glasgow
52 Provost Ross's House, Aberdeen
53 St Kilda
54 Souter Johnnie's Cottage, Kirkoswald
55 Strome Ferry
56 Threave Gardening School
57 Torridon Estate
58 Turret House, Kelso
59 Weaver's Cottage, Kilbarchan

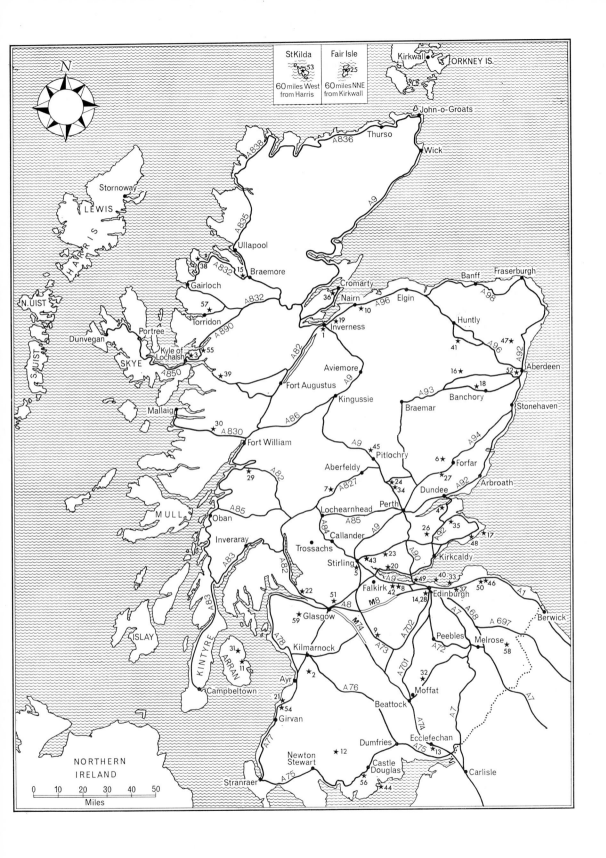

StKilda
★53
60 miles West
from Harris

Fair Isle
★25
60 miles NNE
from Kirkwall

Kirkwall
ORKNEY IS.

John-o-Groats

A836
Thurso
Wick

A838

A836

LEWIS
Stornoway

HARRIS

A835

Ullapool

★38 A832 15 Braemore
Gairloch

57
★ Torridon

N.UIST

A832

A96
36 Nairn
Cromarty

Banff Fraserburgh

A98

N. UIST

Portree

Dunvegan

SKYE

Kyle of
Lochalsh ★3 55

A890

★19 Inverness
1

★10 Elgin

Huntly
41

A96 47★

A92

A82

Aviemore

A9

16 ★

52★ Aberdeen

Fort Augustus

Kingussie

A93

★18
Banchory

Stonehaven

39

A850

A830

30 A830

A86

Braemar

A94

Fort William

A9

★45
Pitlochry

6 ★ Forfar

27

Arbroath

Mallaig

29

A82

Aberfeldy

7 ★ A827

★24
★34

A92

Dundee

4 ★

MULL

A85

Oban

Lochearnhead

Perth

Callander
A85

26 ★

A92 35★
48★ 17★

Inveraray

A84

A9

A90

Trossachs

★23

Stirling
5

★43
★20

Kirkcaldy

A83

A82

51
★22

48

Falkirk
42 ★8
A9

49★ 40★33★
37★ 50 46★★
Edinburgh

A1

59 ★ Glasgow

M74

M8

14,28

A7 A68

Berwick

A697

ISLAY

KINTYRE

ARRAN

31★

11★

Ayr ★2

Campbeltown

21
★54
Girvan

A78

Kilmarnock

A77

A73

A701

9

A702

A72

Peebles

Melrose
58★

Moffat
32★

A76

Beattock

A74

A7

A7

Dumfries

Ecclefechan
13★

Newton
Stewart

★12

Castle
Douglas

A75

56★
★44

Carlisle

Stranraer

A75

NORTHERN
IRELAND

0 10 20 30 40 50
Miles

Brodick Castle

The delights of Brodick Castle on the Isle of Arran are many and varied. It has a beautiful setting between the bay and the hills and an incomparable garden; its principal rooms contain a wealth of fine furniture, paintings, china and porcelain; and it has a long, eventful history.

The Vikings appreciated the merits of the site and had a fortress there. Robert the Bruce stayed here in 1306 before returning to the reconquest of Scotland. In the fifteenth century the castle was sacked three times, twice by the English. In Covenanting times it changed hands on several occasions. In the Civil War it was held for Charles II until after the battle of Worcester. During the Commonwealth the medieval castle was enlarged, but it was not again to be the scene of violence. Instead the castle was embellished during the eighteenth and nineteenth centuries with the fine collections which it now contains, and during the 1840's was given a new wing. This addition was an ingenious and successful piece of designing by James Gillespie Graham, the architect of a number of Scotland's country houses and of the Tolbooth Spire in Edinburgh. He contrived to make his new wing harmonize very satisfactorily with the exterior of the older building and, at the same time, to provide the more spacious rooms needed as settings for fine furniture and works of art.

These enlargements and the accumulation of the contents of the castle were the work of the Hamilton family. Their connection with Brodick began early in the sixteenth century by a marriage with the sister of King James III, and it continued till 1958. They garnered an important contribution to the collections in the castle from the great English collector William Beckford of Fonthill. Beckford's daughter married the tenth Duke of Hamilton in 1810. When her father died she inherited some of his magnificent collection of European and oriental porcelain, Flemish ivories, pastoral paintings by Watteau and other treasures.

The gardens, for all that there have been gardens at Brodick at least since the eighteenth century, owe their present great distinction and interest to the late Duchess of Montrose (daughter of the twelfth Duke of Hamilton), who began the creation of the *woodland garden* soon after the 1914–18 war. She brought the vision and skill of a creative artist to the task, and her garden blooms from early spring to late autumn. She took full advantage

Brodick Castle, Isle of Arran: the woodland garden.

of the climate of Arran, which is astonishingly mild and helpful to the gardener, to introduce a variety of shrubs and plants from overseas.

The Trust acquired the castle and grounds in 1958 from the Treasury, who had accepted them in payment of death duty. Endowment towards their upkeep was furnished by public subscription. At the same time Lady Jean Fforde (daughter of Mary, Duchess of Montrose, the creator of the gardens) gave to the Trust eight thousand acres of mountainous country on the island. A note on this property will be found on page 318.

The Isle of Arran: Goatfell, with Brodick Castle below.

Goatfell and Glen Rosa

ISLE OF ARRAN

The Trust's Arran property, which extends to eight thousand acres, includes Glen Rosa, Cir Mhor (2,618 feet) and Goatfell (2,866 feet). Here is fine rock-climbing and ridge-walking. Also, which is encouragement to less adventurous spirits, the Trust's Guide to its Brodick and Arran Hills property concludes with the reflection: 'Despite the rugged nature of the Arran

Brodick Castle, Isle of Arran: the drawing-room.

Hills they are remarkably safe, being low enough to be climbed quickly but high enough to give that authentic feeling of the wild which is one of the great rewards of hill country.'

Given a clear day these hills command sweeping and impressive views to Ireland, to the Lake District and to the western seaboard of Scotland. Their bird population reads like a catalogue of predators: peregrine falcon, merlin, hen-harrier, buzzard, sparrow-hawk, kestrel and, for good measure, not only the short-eared owl, a daytime hunter, but also the golden eagle. The golden eagle was for a time extinct in Arran but is now re-established.

This property was given to the Trust in 1958 by Lady Jean Fforde at the time when *Brodick Castle* and the garden which her mother had created there were also acquired.

Hugh Miller's Cottage

CROMARTY

The seventeenth-century thatched cottage in which Hugh Miller was born is one of the buildings which are preserved by the Trust rather for their association with some famous Scotsman than for their architectural interest. (*Carlyle's Birthplace* and *Barrie's* also come into this category, as does the *Bachelors' Club* at Tarbolton.)

Miller, who was born in the cottage in October 1802, was a man of great versatility. He was a stonemason by trade. He was for a time accountant in the Commercial Bank of Cromarty. As a man of letters, he contributed to Mackay Wilson's *Tales of the Borders*. He also gained wide recognition as a geologist. The cottage now houses a small museum.

The cottage was given to the Trust by the Cromarty Town Council in 1938.

Inverewe

WESTER ROSS

The garden of Inverewe in Wester Ross was begun just over a hundred years ago, not on the site of an earlier garden, nor in an area where exotic plants already flourished. Quite to the contrary: Mrs Mairi T. Sawyer wrote of the place her father, Osgood Mackenzie, chose that it was almost devoid of vegetation; that the only soil was acid black peat and that the exposed position caught nearly every gale that blows. But in conclusion she wrote: 'To counter the more vicious of the elements there is the benevolent warm flow of air emanating from the Gulf Stream.'

So, supported by the Gulf Stream and an annual rainfall of sixty inches, and armed with both a love of trees and flowers and a knowledge of the coast (his father and grandfather had been Lairds of Gairloch), Osgood Mackenzie began in 1862 to make the garden which today delights visitors from all over the world with its profusion of exotic plants.

Frost is not entirely unknown at Inverewe—indeed the Fahrenheit thermometers showed twenty-five degrees below freezing-point in early 1947

Inverewe,
Ross and Cromarty:
view of
Ben Airrdh Char
from the
walled garden.

Hugh Miller's
Cottage,
Ross and Cromarty:
birthplace of the
geologist.

The Peaks of Kintail: Loch Duich in the foreground, Ross and Cromarty.

and during the winter of 1954–5—but it is unusual, and Mrs Sawyer was able to claim that her father could grow 'as many and as good plants at Inverewe in the open air as is possible at Kew under glass'.

Establishing them called for windbreaks, the physical importation of soil, and time. Mackenzie planted Corsican pine and Scots fir as his windbreak with a variety of other trees in support. His daughter has recorded that: 'To Corsican pine he awarded first prize for rapidity of growth on bad soil and exposed sites and confessed that among the trees, many of the foreigners were far and away hardier than most Scottish natives.'

After about fifteen years Mackenzie felt he was making real progress and introduced eucalyptus and Monterey pine. Some of these trees have now grown to a great size, and twining on them are creepers introduced from many parts of the world. The general layout of the garden is informal, winding paths leading from section to section. The names of some of the sections are self-explanatory, thus: 'Grove of Big Trees' and 'Azaleas', but others, like 'Peace Plot' and 'Bambooselem', need explanation. 'Peace Plot' is a post-

1914–18 war planting of the more tender rhododendrons. 'Bambooselem' covers not only bamboos but also massed hydrangeas and a twenty-eight-foot-high *Magnolia stellata*.

The Trust's guide to Inverewe, edited by D. J. Macqueen Cowan, former assistant keeper of the Royal Botanic Garden in Edinburgh, includes a list of what he describes as 'the more noteworthy plants and flowers to be found in the garden'. This list totals no less than 320 items.

Mrs Sawyer, who for many years helped her father at Inverewe and after his death in 1922 continued the work which he had set in hand, gave the garden to the Trust, with endowment for upkeep, in 1952. This endowment was added to by the Pilgrim Trust and an anonymous donor.

Kintail, Balmacara, the Falls of Glomach

WESTER ROSS

The Trust has three large properties in Wester Ross, Kintail of fifteen thousand acres, Balmacara of eight thousand and the Falls of Glomach of two thousand. They preserve a magnificent stretch of West Highland scenery embracing the Five Sisters of Kintail, which rise abruptly from the lochside to three thousand feet, most of the Kyle-Plockton peninsula, and the 370-foot Falls of Glomach.

Kintail is a perfect countryside for climbers and for hill walkers, and the Trust's property is freely open to them at all times of the year. The walker here is rewarded not only by magnificent views but in early summer also by a wealth of bird life—from meadow pipits to the golden eagle. The Falls of Glomach, the highest in Britain, are remote and difficult of approach and live up to their name—Glomach being in Gaelic 'forbidding'. The water sweeps down a high wild glen before making its abrupt drop, to be splintered on a rock projection three hundred feet below and fall again to the bottom pool. Balmacara is a well wooded property and shows some exceptionally fine Douglas firs. Balmacara House has been leased to the education authority for special schools.

The Kintail estate was given to the Trust in 1944 by the late Mr P. J. H. Unna; the Balmacara estate was bequeathed in 1946 by the late Lady Hamilton; the Falls of Glomach were given in 1941 by Mrs B. C. M. Douglas of Killilan and Captain the Hon. Gerald Portman of Inverinate.

The Torridon Estate and Alligin Shuas

ROSS AND CROMARTY

The fourteen-thousand-acre Torridon estate includes some of the finest mountain scenery in Scotland. The north-western boundary of the estate runs along the summit ridge of Beinn Eighe (3,309 feet); to the south is the great mass of Liathach (3,546 feet), its seven tops linked by narrow ridges nearly five miles long; and to the west the mountain of Beinn Alligin (3,232 feet). In addition to their scenic beauty the mountains hold great interest for geologists.

There is a diversity of wild life on the estate, including red deer, pine marten, wild cat, golden eagle, peregrine falcon and seals.

The estate, less the mansion-house and adjacent woods, was given to the Trust in 1967 by the Treasury, who had accepted it in payment of death duty following the death of the fourth Earl of Lovelace. During his last few years the earl had been in consultation with the Trust and others with a view to arranging for public access to the Torridon Mountains.

The Trust now also owns Alligin Shuas, two thousand acres which adjoin the western extremity of the Torridon estate and were formerly part of it. This was given, by their three sons in Montreal, in memory of Sir Charles and Lady Edith Gordon. Sir Charles was owner of the whole Torridon estate from 1927 to 1947.

Abertarff House, Inverness

INVERNESS-SHIRE

Abertarff House (page 327) is one of the oldest houses in the burgh of Inverness, dating from the sixteenth century.

The Trust received it as a gift from the National Commercial Bank of Scotland in 1963, and during the next three years restored it and improved the interior to modern standards. The restoration work was given a Civic Trust award. The house has been let to An Comunn Gaidhealach (The Highland Association), and is used as its northern headquarters.

Torridon, Ross and Cromarty, looking across Upper Loch Torridon to the Torridon mountains.

Plockton Village, Loch Carron and the hills of Applecross, Ross and Cromarty.

Culloden, Inverness-shire: Old Leanach Farmhouse.

Culloden

INVERNESS-SHIRE

In the 1930's it was feared that commercial development would encroach on the battlefield and its surroundings. This fear prompted the late Mr Alexander Munro of Leanach Farm to give two pieces of the battlefield to

Abertarff House, Inverness.

the Trust. Gifts from others (including the late Hector Forbes of Culloden) have followed, and the Trust now has in its care the graves of the Clans, the Memorial Cairn, the Well of the Dead, the Cumberland Stone and *Old Leanach Farmhouse.*

Old Leanach Farmhouse, illustrated on page 326, a silent witness of the battle, is now used as an information centre for visitors to the battlefield.

327

Glenfinnan Monument near Fort William, Inverness-shire, looking down Loch Shiel.

Glenfinnan Monument

INVERNESS-SHIRE

A tall tower topped by a statue of a kilted highlander stands within a grassy enclosure at the head of Loch Shiel. On the walls of the enclosure are inscriptions in Gaelic, Latin and English recording that the monument was erected in 1815 by Alexander Macdonald of Glenadale on the spot where Prince Charles Edward raised his standard on 19th August 1745.

Entrance to Glencoe, Argyllshire, showing Bidean Nam Bean.

This Alexander was a grandson of the Alexander Macdonald of Glenadale at whose house the prince stayed on the night before the raising of the standard.

The statue, which is the work of the sculptor Greenshields, is not a statue of the prince himself but a figure representative of the men who followed him. There is a staircase inside the tower which gives access to the top platform.

The monument was given to the Trust in 1938 by Sir Walter Blount, the Trustees of Glenadale Estates and the Roman Catholic diocese of Argyll and the Isles.

The preservation of the monument represents an important side of the Trust's work, namely the preservation of places with historic associations. In this same category other Trust properties are the *Pass of Killiecrankie, Bannockburn Monument* and *Culloden.*

Glencoe, Argyllshire, looking south across Loch Leven towards the north end of Glencoe.

Glencoe and Dalness

ARGYLLSHIRE

In Glencoe and Dalness the Trust owns 12,800 acres of rugged mountain country. Included in the property are Buachaille Etive Mor and *Bidean Nam Bean*, which is the highest peak in Argyll (3,766 feet). There is access for walkers and climbers, and the Trust opens an information centre in Glencoe village from May to mid October. The property was bought in 1935 and 1937 to prevent commercial exploitation, the money for the purchase being provided by the combined efforts of the Scottish Mountaineering,

Alpine and other climbing clubs, the Pilgrim Trust and a public subscription.

These Glencoe and Dalness properties make up a rough triangle, each side about six miles long, between the River Etive above Dalness and the River Coe above Clachaig. The Trust has published a useful guide to the area, which has a particularly interesting and helpful section on the hill walking for which the area provides the most glorious scope.

The scene of the massacre in 1692 is not on the Trust property.

The Grey Mare's Tail

DUMFRIESSHIRE

The Grey Mare's Tail, which is the Tail Burn flowing from Loch Skeen just before it enters Moffat Water, is a two-hundred-foot waterfall (page 332). Here the Trust acquired in 1962 a property of rather more than two thousand acres. It harbours rare flowers and, occasionally, some wild goats.

Craigievar Castle

ABERDEENSHIRE

twenty-six miles west of Aberdeen, five miles north of Lumphanan

In the scholarly yet racy guide to Craigievar (pages 334–5) which Dr Douglas Simpson wrote for the Trust he describes it as 'the most cultured, scholarly and refined' of all Scotland's many castles, and 'a masterpiece of old-time Scottish architecture'. Less learned visitors find it easy to agree with these superlatives.

It was finished in 1626 and remains virtually unaltered. It is impressively sited high up on a hillside. The lower walls are solid and plain and above there is a rich array of corbelling, turrets and cupolas. For the most part the design and decoration of the exterior come from native origins but there are also, as the balustrade on one of the towers, elements brought in from abroad. The

The Grey Mare's Tail, Birkhill, Dumfriesshire.

Leith Hall, Aberdeenshire.

interior, though largely medieval in its plan, has superb plasterwork, of the style used to decorate Elizabethan houses.

The castle was built by William Forbes, who had made a fortune as a merchant in trade with Danzig. He was a graduate of Edinburgh University and a man of culture. It is not known who assisted him in the design and building of Craigievar, but it is thought probable that he employed a master mason named I. Bel who is known to have worked in Aberdeenshire at the relevant time.

In 1963, following a public appeal, the Trust bought the castle from the trustees of the late Lord Sempill. A start was also made on building up an endowment fund, for which donations are still sought, for its permanent preservation.

Craigievar Castle, Aberdeenshire.

Craigievar Castle, Aberdeenshire: the Great Hall.

Leith Hall

seven miles south of Huntly on A 979

Leith Hall (page 333) is built round a courtyard. It was not designed as a whole but reached its present size and plan by stages as succeeding generations of the Leith family made their additions. The oldest parts are in the north wing and date from 1650. Much of the building was done during the eighteenth century. When James Leith began the Hall which was to be their home for the next three hundred years, the Leith family had been landholders in Aberdeenshire since the fourteenth century. The Hall contains many family and Jacobite relics.

The name of Hay was added to that of Leith when in 1789 General Alexander Leith inherited the Rannes estates from his great-uncle Andrew Hay. Andrew Hay had been an ardent Jacobite, 'out' in the '45 rising, and was excluded from the Act of Indemnity. He persisted in seeking a pardon and eventually this was granted. It is on view in the Hall; reputedly the only Jacobite pardon extant. Many of the family soldiered with distinction, notably Sir James Leith Hay, who commanded the 5th Division in the Peninsular War and was buried (in 1816) in Westminster Abbey. Charles Leith Hay, last male representative of the main line of the family, was killed in 1939 while serving as an officer in the Royal Artillery. Leith Hall, with twelve hundred acres of farm and woodland, was given to the Trust by his mother, the Hon. Mrs Leith Hay of Rannes, in 1945.

Pitmedden

ABERDEENSHIRE

Pitmedden Garden near Udny was designed in 1675. At that time the fashion was still for a formal garden, even if it were a large one with a variety of plants. As Miles Hadfield writes in an appendix to the Trust's guide-book to Pitmedden, 'the simple knot had been elaborated into the freely designed baroque parterre'.

Pitmedden Garden,
near Udny, Aberdeenshire.
Below : An aerial
view.

Alexander Seton, an eminent lawyer by profession, had studied the gardens at Holyrood House and other great houses. When he came to build a mansion-house on the site of the old castle of Pitmedden—his family had acquired the estate in 1603—he made his own plan for the garden. His descendants continued in possession of the estate till 1894, when it was bought at auction by Alexander Keith. The garden had not been maintained and had declined to the status of a kitchen garden. Alexander's son, Major James Keith, made improvements and in 1952 gave it to the Trust with sixty-five acres of the estate and an endowment. Since then it has been brought into being again as the garden of parterres and heraldic patterns which Alexander Seton made there.

This reconstruction has required much ingenuity as well as labour. No detailed plan of Seton's garden survived, as many papers were destroyed in a fire at Pitmedden in 1818; but strategically placed, surviving yew trees provided a guide to layout and Seton's garden pavilions were there to be repaired. Miles of box hedge have been replanted: literally miles, as planting in one year alone (1956) amounted to two miles. Colour is provided by thirty thousand annuals, raised under glass at Pitmedden. Of the four parterres one is now devoted to Alexander Seton and his family and the others are modelled on those of the garden at Holyrood House as shown by James Gordon of Rothiemay, since it is believed that Seton consulted their designer.

Crathes Castle

KINCARDINESHIRE

fourteen miles west of Aberdeen, on the north bank of the Dee

Crathes Castle—apart from the east wing which was added on during the eighteenth century as an enlargement to the building—was built between 1546 and 1596. It has been lived in continuously ever since, and retains not only its original interior decoration but also some of its original furniture.

It was built by the Burnett family, who had held land here on the River Dee at least since 1323. Shown in the castle today is the jewelled ivory horn reputedly given by King Robert the Bruce to Alexander Burnett in that year, with lands at Crathes and a duty to serve as coroner of the Royal Forest of Drum. It was his descendants who built the sixteenth-century castle, made the eighteenth-century additions to the building, and laid out the fine, formal eighteenth-century garden which has been maintained and

Crathes Castle, Kincardineshire.

improved and remains one of the attractions of Crathes. Though mindful
of their family home, they were not always a stay-at-home family, and at
different times provided Basle with a professor of philosophy and Salisbury
with a bishop. During the eighteenth century a William Burnett was
successively governor of New York and of New Jersey, Massachusetts and
New Hampshire, and it is after him that the Burnett Society in America is
named. In 1951 the late Sir James Burnett of Leys gave Crathes to the Trust
with an endowment.

The castle is a four-storey building with six-foot-thick walls, but is far
from being plain and forbidding, since it is topped with square and rounded
turrets and has dormer windows and gargoyles.

Crathes Castle, Kincardineshire: tempera painted ceiling, one of the Nine Nobles.

Inside, apart from the interest of an interior which has been preserved as its sixteenth-century creators made it, there is the very special interest of the *tempera painted ceilings*. These were part of the original decoration and the painting is among the most beautiful in Scotland. With the tempera technique (which entails using egg-yolk as a binding agent for chalk colours) the medieval craftsman was able to achieve unusually bright colours. These remain, but the paintings present other problems of preservation, those at Crathes having been subject to a certain amount of flaking. But the Trust (which has similar paintings to care for in the chapel of *Falkland Palace*, in *Gladstones Land* in Edinburgh and at *Culross*) became engaged on a programme

340

of research and experiment which has led to the establishment of a centre for restoration of tempera and other works at *Stenhouse Mansion*, Edinburgh, which it is hoped will establish a satisfactory method of treatment.

Of the three painted ceilings at Crathes one carries a miscellaneous assembly of figures; but the others each have an ambitious theme, vigorously executed. One shows the Nine Nobles—the stock pagan, Old Testament and Christian heroes of the troubadours' repertoire—each with a eulogistic rhyme. The other is the Chamber of the Nine Muses, where in addition to the figures of the four muses the painter has added figures for five virtues to make up his set of nine.

The gardens were given their formal plan at the beginning of the eighteenth century. Lime avenues were planted leading to the river, and yew hedges, now grown to twelve feet, were established to mark the division of the garden into rectangular sections. The various divisions of the garden have now been planted with a very great variety of shrubs and plants, some native and others from North and South America, Africa, India and New Zealand.

Kirkwynd Cottages, Glamis

ANGUS

———— ⌐ ⌐ ————

This row of seventeenth-century cottages with stone-slabbed roofs (page 343) was restored by the Trust in 1957 and converted into a museum. They now house the very fine Angus Folk Collection.

Barrie's Birthplace, Kirriemuir

ANGUS

———— ⌐ ⌐ ————

No. 9 Brechin Road (page 343), is a modest two-storey house in a corner of the town known as the Tenements. James Barrie was born in it in 1860 and lived there until he was eight. In the small communal wash-house behind the house he staged his first play—reputedly a drama with a finale in which the actors struggled to push one another into the boiler.

341

Ben Lawers, Perthshire, seen from a point west of Killin, looking north-east.

Opposite: Kirkwynd Cottages, Glamis.
Barrie's Birthplace, Kirriemuir, Angus.

Barrie wrote much of his home town—which he named Thrums after the loose threads used by the handloom weavers there to mend broken threads in their looms. His father was a handloom weaver, and at the time of Barrie's birth worked a loom in a downstairs room in the house. As the family grew, he moved it to a loom shop. Barrie always held a great love for Kirriemuir, revisited it in the years of his success, and in accordance with his wishes was buried in the cemetery there.

The house and wash-house have been restored and personal possessions and mementoes of the playwright and his family have been collected there.

The house was given to the Trust in 1937 by Mr D. Alves of Caernarvon. He had bought it in that year on hearing rumours that it was to be shipped to America as a Barrie museum and the wash-house taken to London and re-erected in Kensington Gardens.

Killin, Perthshire: the bridge over the River Dochart, Ben Lawers in the background.

344

Ben Lawers

On the southern slopes of Ben Lawers (page 342) and the nearby Ben Ghlas and Coire Odhar the Trust now has an eight-thousand-acre property. Ben Lawers rises to 3,984 feet—the highest mountain in Perthshire—and many rare alpine plants grow there. From the summit there are views of both the Atlantic and the North Sea. A Nature Trail has been established on Ben Lawers and an information hut is maintained at a car park there during the summer months. Coire Odhar is popular for winter sports. The property was bought in 1950 from the Trust's Mountainous Country Fund —a fund formed by Mr P. J. H. Unna.

The Trust has published an extremely interesting and informative book on Ben Lawers containing expert accounts of its history, plant and animal life and the skiing areas in the range. In his notes on its plant ecology Dr Duncan Poore of the Nature Conservancy describes Ben Lawers as far famed for the richness of its alpine flora and rightly called 'the botanists' Mecca'. To this the Trust's introduction to the book adds a rider that one of the main objects in acquiring Ben Lawers was to ensure the preservation of the rare alpine flora and urging visitors not to uproot and 'collect' these flowers as specimens.

Mr Unna, who died in a climbing accident near Dalmally in 1950, was a president of the Scottish Mountaineering Club in the 1930's. His generosity and his active interest have enabled the Trust to acquire or to accept *Glencoe and Dalness*, *Kintail*, Ben Lawers and *Torridon*.

Dunkeld

The Trust has achieved an excellent work of preservation and restoration at Dunkeld (page 347). In the early 1950's almost all the charming *little houses* between Atholl Street and the cathedral, dating from the rebuilding of the town after the battle of Dunkeld (1689), were half derelict and being considered for demolition. Between 1954 and 1966 the Trust restored twenty of these houses and the Perth County Council another twenty. The charm of the exteriors has been retained while the interiors have been improved to modern standards. The Trust was enabled to carry out this work by receiving most of the property as a gift from the Atholl Estates and by the response to a public appeal for funds to pay for its restoration. See also the Little Houses, Fife, page 355.

The Hermitage

PERTHSHIRE

The Hermitage, near Dunkeld (page 351), also once called Ossian's Hall, was the centre-piece of an eighteenth-century garden and sited to command a dramatic view of the waterfall below. It was built by the third Duke of Atholl in 1758 and decorated inside in 1783 with paintings of Hospitality, supported by Justice, and Fortitude and Harmony, attended by Temperance and Prudence. It suffered damage from vandalism during the nineteenth century but was restored, in simplified form, by the Trust in 1952 as the centre-piece of a delightful walk through the woods along the River Braan. Together with fifty acres of the woodland it was given to the Trust in 1943, in accordance with the wishes of the eighth Duke, by his widow.

Pass of Killiecrankie

PERTHSHIRE

The Pass of Killiecrankie (page 348–9) ranks for preservation as well for its beauty as for its historical association. The viewpoint towards the head of the Pass has long been admired by visitors, among them Queen Victoria, who came here in 1844.

The site of the battle of 27th July 1689 was the hillside above the main road a mile north of the Pass. But it was through the Pass that King William's men advanced to engage the Jacobite army led by 'Bonnie Dundee', and through it that many of them later fled in retreat.

The Trust property of fifty acres here was given in 1947 by Mrs Edith Foster.

Dunkeld, Perthshire: little houses.

Pass of Killiecrankie, Perthshire: the railway viaduct over the River Garry.

Pass of Killiecrankie, Perthshire: the River Garry.

Bannockburn, Stirling: statue of the Bruce.

Bannockburn Monument

STIRLINGSHIRE

The battle area has for the most part been built on. But about sixty acres around the Borestone were bought for preservation in 1930 and later given to the Trust. The purchase in 1930 was made from a public subscription which was raised by a national committee led by the Earl of Elgin, head of

The Hermitage, near Dunkeld, Perthshire.

the Bruce family. According to tradition the Borestone site was Bruce's command post before the battle, and takes its name from a large stone block with a socket in which it is said that he placed his standard. Only fragments remain.

On the 24th June 1964, the 650th anniversary of the battle, Her Majesty the Queen unveiled the statue of King Robert the Bruce which now stands on the site.

The statue, a bronze by C. d'O. Pilkington Jackson, was presented to the Trust by the King Robert the Bruce Memorial Fund Committee which had commissioned it.

An information centre, operated by the Trust in association with the Royal Burgh of Stirling, has been established beside the main road.

Falkland Palace, Fife: seventeenth-century Dutch bed in the King's Room; workmanship comparable to that of furnishing of Stuart royal bedrooms.

Falkland Palace

FIFE

Although no sovereign has lived at Falkland since Charles II and the Palace has been in the custody of hereditary keepers, it is still the property of the sovereign. In 1952 the present hereditary keeper (Major Michael Crichton-Stuart) appointed the National Trust for Scotland to be deputy keeper and

Falkland Palace, Fife: the Chapel Royal.

made over to the Trust an endowment for future maintenance of palace and gardens.

There were earlier buildings on the site but the Palace, which has been in part restored during the last eighty years, was built in the mid-fifteenth century and enlarged and improved about 1540. It was a hunting palace of many of the Stuarts, including James V and Mary Queen of Scots. James V made the sixteenth-century improvements in the palace in part, it seems, to welcome his French bride. He also had a tennis court built, the only real-tennis court in Scotland.

Charles II in 1650, on practically his last visit to Falkland, gave new colours to the troops selected to guard him. This is now considered to have been the christening of the Scots Guards. The regiment has retained a connection with Falkland. In 1958 it mounted guard when, on the occasion of the quincentenary of the royal burgh, the Queen visited there.

Misfortune occurred in 1653 when the East Range of the palace was burned, apparently by accident not design, during the occupation of the town and palace by Cromwellian troops.

During the eighteenth century and until 1855 maintenance of the fabric was neglected and the palace became ruinous. The hereditary keeper of that date, on the advice of Sir Walter Scott, began to restore it as a 'romantic ruin'. But in 1877 John Crichton-Stuart, third Marquess of Bute, became

The Giles, Pittenweem, Fife, restored under the Trust's Little Houses scheme.

Nos. 5 and 6 Rumford, Crail, Fife, restored under the Trust's Little Houses scheme.

hereditary keeper and set about the full restoration of the Gatehouse. His policy has been maintained, and today not only the Gatehouse has been restored but also the finely decorated *Chapel Royal*, and the *King's Room*, in the East Range, has been redecorated and refurnished. Since 1945 the Palace Garden has been re-created.

Beside the Palace Gatehouse is St Andrew's House, once occupied by a member of the royal household. This was restored and given to the Trust in 1952 by Major Michael Crichton-Stuart.

Little Houses, Pittenweem and Crail

FIFE

In 1960 the Trust formed a Little Houses Restoration Fund. This is being used to preserve the charm and individuality which many Scots burghs derive from their domestic architecture. Old houses of interest are bought, reconstructed to modern living standards and sold under safeguards—the proceeds of the sale being then available for another reconstruction. The illustrations on page 354 show what had once been two small seventeenth-century houses in an advanced state of disrepair now restored and made into one family-size house that complies with modern standards of comfort, and a block of seventeenth-century houses after reconstruction. Similar restorations have been carried out or are in progress in six other towns including *Dunkeld* (see page 345) and *Culross*.

The Binns

WEST LOTHIAN

three and a half miles east of Linlithgow on A 904

The site has been inhabited, traditionally, since Pictish times, but the house of the Binns (page 356) now is substantially early seventeenth-century, with some additional rooms acquired in the middle of the eighteenth century, and battlements early in the nineteenth century. The battlements were substituted

The Binns,
West Lothian.

A moulded plaster
ceiling in
the Binns.

for crow-stepping and pointed turrets. Four of the main rooms have very fine ornate *plaster ceilings* that date from 1612 to 1630. It has not been established whether this beautiful work was carried out by Italians or by Italian-trained Scots, though there is good evidence that the latter were concerned in it.

In 1944, when Eleanor Dalyell of the Binns gave it to the Trust, the house had been the home of the Dalyells for more than three hundred years. Included in the contents of the building, which formed part of her gift, are a number of interesting family portraits. Among those portrayed is the builder of the house, Thomas Dalyell. He had accompanied James VI to London in 1603 and there made such a fortune that on his return to Scotland nine years later, he was able to buy the Binns and enlarge and transform the house. Also, there is his son, the famous General Tam Dalyell of the Binns. It was in 1681, while he was commander-in-chief of the forces in Scotland, that the regiment which became known as the Royal Scots Greys was formed and held its first musters at the Binns. Succeeding generations of the family have given loyal and gallant service in the armed forces of the Crown, and Sir John Graham Dalyell, author of works on a variety of subjects, was knighted in 1836 for his services to literature and science.

Phantassie Doocot, East Linton

EAST LOTHIAN

Phantassie Doocot, as the illustration on page 359 shows, is a highly picturesque building. Its round walls, which are four feet thick at the base, project upwards to a horseshoe embracing the roof and giving the 'doos' a sheltered southern exposure. It has been suggested that the builder got his idea for the design from southern France. It has nesting-places for five hundred birds. The date of its building is not known, but many 'dowcots', as they were then known, were built during the sixteenth century, as an Act of 1503 required lords and lairds to make such provision for food supply. By 1617 so many had been built that they had become an embarrassment to the authorities. So, the latter announced that because of 'the frequent building of doucottis by all manner of personnes', the privilege would be restricted to those owning a specified amount of land.

357

Hamilton House, Prestonpans, East Lothian.

Hamilton House, Prestonpans

EAST LOTHIAN

Hamilton House was scheduled for demolition in 1937 under a road-widening scheme, but was later reprieved and acquired by the Trust.

It was built in 1628 by John Hamilton, who is referred to as a prosperous Edinburgh burgess. It has had two tastes of military life, having been used as a barracks while there was the threat of a Napoleonic invasion, and earlier (by repute), occupied by Prince Charles Edward's troops after the battle of Prestonpans.

Edinburgh,
Charlotte Square.

Phantassie Doocot,
East Linton,
East Lothian.

Preston Mill, East Linton

EAST LOTHIAN

—∙—

Preston Mill on the River Tyne is a delightfully picturesque group of buildings and it is a subject much favoured by artists. It is also a working mill,
being (it is believed) the oldest water-mill in Scotland which is still in
operation. The machinery was renovated for the Trust a few years ago by
Messrs Joseph Rank Ltd. In addition to the mill building itself, the photo-
graph on page 361 shows the grain-drying kiln. This is the building with the
conical roof, which looks as though it might, perhaps, be an oast house. It is
connected to the mill by a stairway. The grain is dried by underfloor heating,
and the cowl at the top of the roof turns with the wind to clear the smoke.
Its projecting rudder is known locally as the Long Arm of Friendship.

The mill was given to the Trust in 1950 by the trustees of the late Mr
John Gray and money for restoration work raised through a public appeal.

Nos. 5–7 Charlotte Square, Edinburgh

MIDLOTHIAN

—∙—

These houses (page 359) are on the north side of a square designed by Robert
Adam in 1792 and, so far at least as the north side is concerned, completed
almost exactly as he intended. It is easy for layman and expert alike to endorse
Sir Basil Spence's verdict on one of the finest squares in Europe: 'It is here
that we find civic architecture at its best, created by a master.'

Nos. 5, 6 and 7 were accepted by the Treasury in part payment of death
duty on the estate of the fifth Marquess of Bute and given to the Trust in 1966.

No. 5, of which the National Trust for Scotland has been tenant since
1950, is the headquarters of the Trust. Nos. 6 and 7 have been let—No. 6
to a group of distinguished Scots who are collectively the Bute Trustees and
have renamed it Bute House. They intend to furnish it as the official residence
of the Secretary of State for Scotland.

Preston Mill, East Linton, East Lothian.

Turret House, Kelso, Roxburghshire.

Turret House, Kelso

ROXBURGHSHIRE

Turret House, though altered and enlarged during the eighteenth and nineteenth centuries, was probably built in the seventeenth to contain two or perhaps three sets of apartments.

It was restored by the Trust in 1965 with the co-operation of St Andrew's Episcopal Church, Kelso, to whom it is now leased as a church hall.

362

Provan Hall, Glasgow

LANARKSHIRE

Provan Hall, near Stepps (page 364), built in the fifteenth century, is probably the most perfectly preserved pre-Reformation mansion-house in Scotland.

It was given to the Trust in 1935 by a group of people who also had the building restored.

Bachelors' Club, Tarbolton

AYRSHIRE

Among Trust properties associated with famous Scotsmen there are two associated with Robert Burns—*Souter Johnnie's Cottage* in Kirkoswald and the Bachelors' Club in Tarbolton. The club was formed about 1780, and for their meetings Burns and his friends used the small stone house dating from the seventeenth century which is illustrated on page 364. It is said that Burns became a Freemason here. The Trust acquired the property in 1938. It now contains a small museum.

Culzean Castle

AYRSHIRE

ten miles south-west of Ayr

The Trust's guide-book to Culzean (page 365) refers to the castle's 'romantic shell and Georgian interior'. That is a classic example of the understatement which tersely points towards the whole glorious truth.

Culzean stands on the site of a medieval castle. It would be hard to find

Provan Hall, near Stepps, Glasgow, Lanarkshire.
Bachelors' Club, Tarbolton, Ayrshire.

Culzean Castle, Ayrshire.

a more romantic natural setting or more beautiful man-made approaches. The transformation of the old castle and the design and decoration of its 'Georgian interior' was no routine exercise by eighteenth-century craftsmen, but the work of Robert Adam himself.

About 1770, just before the work of transformation began, Culzean belonged to the ninth Earl of Cassillis, whose family (the Kennedys) had played their part in many warlike encounters since medieval times. The ninth Earl's interests lay in peaceful pursuits. He was active in improving standards of farming on his estate, and made some additions to the old castle. His brother, who succeeded him in 1775, employed Adam first to reconstruct the old castle internally, then to build a brew-house and later to demolish the seaward side of the castle and build it anew. Adam's brew-house was replaced a hundred years later by the present west wing, which accords satisfactorily with the older parts of the building.

While at work on the castle itself Adam also designed the archway and viaduct at the approach to the castle, and farm buildings in the grounds.

In designing the exterior of Culzean, Adam was concerned to provide his patron not with a strong place capable of withstanding siege, but a

Culzean Castle, Ayrshire: the Round Drawing Room.

romantic, castle-like building of a style then in vogue. He brought to this task both the memory of his youthful study of Scottish traditional styles and all that he had seen of castles in Italy.

For the interior he designed a grand central staircase with elaborate gilt balusters and large columns. This links all the great apartments on the first two storeys.

In the 'Eating Room' (since converted to being the Library), the *Round Drawing Room* and the Long Drawing Room, he exercised to the full his genius for decoration. Ceilings, fireplaces and mirrors and other fittings are to his design.

In the grounds of the castle, the walled garden was established in the 1780's. This is devoted partly to roses and subtropical plants and partly to flowers, peaches and other fruits. The rest of the grounds were laid out during the earlier part of the eighteenth century. A profusion of flowers border the Avenues; there is a Camellia House and other ornamental garden buildings.

Culzean remained in the possession of the Kennedy family during the nineteenth century, the twelfth Earl of Cassillis being created Marquess of Ailsa in 1831. His great-grandson (the third Marquess of Ailsa) carried out the Victorian changes in the castle and improved the gardens, establishing rare trees and shrubs there. In 1945 the fifth Marquess gave the castle and 565 acres to the Trust.

In 1946 a flat in the castle was put at the disposal of the late ex-President Dwight D. Eisenhower as a token of Scotland's thanks for his services as Supreme Commander of the Allied Forces in the Second World War.

Souter Johnnie's Cottage, Kirkoswald, Ayrshire: figures of Souter Johnnie and the innkeeper's wife.

Souter Johnnie's Cottage, Kirkoswald

AYRSHIRE

The thatched house now known as Souter Johnnie's Cottage (page 367) was built in 1785 by John Davidson, the village cobbler of Kirkoswald, and he lived in it for the next twenty years. Burns knew Davidson well and took him as prototype for Souter Johnnie in *Tam O'Shanter*.

The house has been furnished with contemporary furniture, including things used by the Souter's family and a cobbler's chair that was almost certainly his, and with Burns relics.

In the garden are life-size *stone figures* of Souter Johnnie and other characters from *Tam O'Shanter* which were carved in 1802 and exhibited in various parts of Scotland and England before being brought to the cottage in 1924.

Appendix

——◦——

Properties not illustrated

Properties which are not illustrated and are not referred to in the notes that accompany the illustrations are noted below.

Restrictive Agreements

In addition to property owned, the Trust for Scotland has Restrictive Agreements over lands in Kirkcudbright and other counties, and over several houses of architectural importance. (See note in Introduction.)

Properties under the guardianship of the Ministry of Works

Arrangements have been made for several properties to be placed in the guardianship of the Ministry of Works. These are:

The Stones of Clava near Culloden Moor in Inverness-shire. Stone circles dating from about 1600 B.C.

In Culross the 'Palace', which was built around 1600 and has decorative painted interior woodwork.

Castle Campbell near Alloa in Clackmannanshire dates from late in the fifteenth century.

Scotstarvit Tower near Cupar, Fife, a fine seventeenth-century tower.

Threave Castle, Kirkcudbrightshire, a fourteenth-century Douglas stronghold on Threave Island in the River Dee.

Other properties are as follows

ROSS AND CROMARTY

Braemore, Wester Ross: Corrieshalloch Gorge, a spectacular mile-long gorge and the 150-foot Falls of Measach.

Inverewe. Inverewe Stage House was an abandoned army camp between Inverewe Garden and Poolewe village. It has now been turned by the Trust and Shell & B.P. (Scotland) Ltd into a caravan and camp site.

Strome Ferry, Wester Ross, ruins of the ancient Strome Castle which was destroyed in 1603.

Morvich Caravan Site, Wester Ross, by Loch Duich on A87. Small camping site (space for 20 caravans) opened 1966.

Fair Isle, Zetland. The most isolated inhabited island in Britain was acquired by the Trust in 1954, with the help of a grant from the Dulverton Trust. Housing and other improvements have been made with a view to retaining the existing population and encouraging new families to settle. A bird observatory was founded here in 1948 by Mr George Waterston. About three hundred species have been noted and there are breeding colonies of great and arctic skuas. Access (twice weekly in summer) by mailboat from Shetland. A hostel for bird-watchers accommodates 14. Apply to warden.

NAIRN

Auldearn, Boath Doocot. Seventeenth-century dovecote on the site of an ancient castle.

ARGYLL

At Burg, Mull, two thousand acres of farmland in south-west Mull.

DUMFRIES

In Ecclefechan, Carlyle's birthplace, the Arched House built by his father and uncle (master masons both) in 1791. It now houses some of Carlyle's letters and belongings. Given by the Carlyle's House Memorial Trust in 1935 at the same time as they gave to the National Trust the house in which he lived in London.

ABERDEEN

In Aberdeen, Shiprow, Provost Ross's House. Built 1593 and the oldest house in Aberdeen. Now the north of Scotland headquarters of the British Council.

PERTHSHIRE

Dunkeld. Stanley Hill, an artificial mound of 1730 given to the Trust in 1958, provides a wooded background to the 'little houses' (page 347).

Craigower and Linn of Tummel. The Trust has two small properties close to Pitlochry in Perthshire. At Craigower, though only thirteen hundred feet up, there is a viewpoint which commands wide views over country typical of the Perthshire highlands. Eleven acres here were given to the Trust in 1947. A mile or so from Craigower, near the Pitlochry–Blair Atholl road, are fifty acres of the banks of the Tummel and the Garry, given to the Trust in 1944. This property adjoins the Trust's property in the Pass of Killiecrankie.

The Linn of Tummel was formerly known as the Falls of Tummel. Development of hydro-electric schemes in the area has taken off some of the Tummel water so the falls can no longer claim to be spectacular, but the river and the woodlands provide a delightful walk.

Perth. Branklyn Garden, a small garden (two acres) with an outstanding collection of plants, particularly alpines. Bequeathed with endowment by Mr John G. Renton, who with his wife made it. The City of Perth is giving practical support in its maintenance.

Menstrie Castle was the birthplace of Sir William Alexander, James VI's Lieutenant for the Plantation of New Scotland, an object furthered by the creation of Nova Scotia baronetcies. The castle is not Trust property, but the latter has had rooms in the castle decorated as Commemoration Rooms. Coats of arms of 107 existing baronets are displayed.

CLACKMANNAN

At Dollar Glen, the paths and bridges which provide attractive walks to the castle were restored after a public appeal for funds in 1950.

FIFE

Balmerino Abbey. Ruins of a thirteenth-century Cistercian monastery.

Culross. In addition to the 'Palace' (under guardianship of the Ministry of Works) the Trust owns other property in Culross. The Study, the Ark and Bishop Leighton's House have been restored. The Study is open at advertised times. Other buildings are being restored as funds permit.

The ruins of St Mungo's Chapel (five miles east of Kincardine off A 985) built 1503 on the traditional site of the saint's birth, were presented to the Trust by the Earl of Elgin in 1947.

Near Cupar, Hill of Tarvit, a late seventeenth-century mansion-house given with its contents and a farming estate. Leased to the Marie Curie Memorial Foundation as a convalescent home.

Kirkcaldy, Sailors' Walk, a harbour-side group of seventeenth-century merchants' houses.

WEST LOTHIAN

Linlithgow, Nos. 44 and 48 High Street. Sixteenth–early seventeenth century. Not open.

South Queensferry, in the main street, Plewlands House. Built 1643. Threatened with demolition. Given to the Trust in 1953. Not open.

MIDLOTHIAN

Edinburgh, Caiy Stone, a nine-foot-high monolith by Oxgangs Road, Fairmilehead, of which no history is known.

Edinburgh. Malleny, Balerno: early seventeenth-century three-storey stone-built house. Garden with herbaceous and shrub borders, yew trees and a doocot which is possibly eighteenth-century. House not open. Given by Mrs Gore-Browne Henderson, with endowment.

Gladstones's Land, No. 483 Lawnmarket, Edinburgh. Built 1620 and originally the home of an Edinburgh burgess, Thomas Gladstones. It has remarkable painted wooden ceilings. Leased to the Saltire Society and used also by the Trust as an information centre.

Stenhouse Mansion, off Stenhouse Road, Edinburgh. An early seventeenth-century merchant's house in which the Trust has now established a centre for the study and restoration of Scottish tempera paintings.

Leith. Lamb's House, Burgess Street. Five-storey merchant's residence and warehouse of about 1600. Now a day centre for Leith Old People's Welfare Council, which helped with its restoration.

Inveresk Lodge, Inveresk. Mainly early seventeenth century. House not open. Garden open.

LANARK

Three miles west of Lanark, Blackhill, Stonebyres, a viewpoint with a commanding view of the Clyde Valley.

DUMBARTON

Bucinch and Ceardoch, two of the thirty islands in Loch Lomond.

On Castlehill, Dumbarton, the cairn erected in 1937 in memory of R. B. Cunninghame Graham. Reputedly on the site of the castle where Robert the Bruce died.

RENFREW

Kilbarchan. Kilbarchan Weaver's Cottage, an eighteenth-century cottage that was used by a hand-loom weaver. Now houses an excellent collection of hand-loom weavers' equipment and types of workmanship.

Port Glasgow. Parklea Farm, a strip of land on the south bank of the Clyde leased to the town council as a recreation ground.

New Galloway, Bruce's Stone, a granite boulder on Moss Raploch where Bruce defeated the English in 1307.

At Rockcliffe, near Dalbeattie; Mote of Mark, the site of an ancient hill fort; on Rough Island a bird sanctuary; and fifty acres of rough coastline between Rockcliffe and Kippford.

At Castle Douglas, the gardens of Threave House, which are open to the public, are used for two-year gardening courses for youths from all over Britain. The house and thirteen-hundred-acre estate were given with endowment in 1948 by the late Major A. F. Gordon of Threave. There has also been established on the estate, on and near the River Dee, a roosting and feeding place for wildfowl. There is controlled access to this Threave Wildfowl Refuge.

ISLE OF GIGHA

On the Isle of Gigha, west of Kintyre, a collection of valuable plants, including rhododendron hybrids.

These are in the garden of Sir James Horlick, who presented them to the Trust in 1962, with an endowment. Under a propagation programme many of the plants are being established in the Trust's own gardens. The Gigha collection is open to visitors during the summer.

LITTLE HOUSES

Some of the work which the Trust has done at Dunkeld, at Crail and at Pittenweem, with the help of the Little Houses Restoration Fund, is the subject of illustrations and notes on pages 345–7 and 354–5. Elsewhere similar work has been completed or is in progress as funds permit. The Trust has summarized the position as showing work completed at Anstruther (The White House, two houses restored as a shop and a flat, St Ayles' Chapel adapted for use as a Fisheries Museum); at Cellardyke (No. 1 Dove Street and No. 1 Harbour Head); at Dysart (The Anchorage; also the Trust is acting as agent for the Commissioners for Crown Estates in the restoration of a group of cottages at the Shore, the first of which is complete); at St Monance, 4–5 West Shore; and at North Berwick, The Lodge, a group of buildings in Quality Street; while further work is in progress or has been planned at Anstruther, Crail, Dysart, Pittenweem and St Monance. At Crail, restoration of the Customs House as a dwelling has been completed.